Poems from the Lollipop Massacre

By J. Martin Strangeweather

All rights reserved. No part of this book may be reproduced or transmitted in any form or by any means, electronic or mechanical, without written permission from the author. All requests should be sent to: jmartinstrangeweather@gmail.com

Cover artwork by J. Martin Strangeweather
Graphic design by Dustin Myers
Published by the Santa Ana Literary Association
Printed in the United States of America
© 2022 by J. Martin Strangeweather

These poems deal with the road behind the music, specifically the North American psychedelic tour scene of the late '80s and early '90s. This was written for all the Deadicated Phans of the world's most dangerous bands.

*for Becky, Ian, Megan, Crystal, Claudio, Jason, Andy,
Daniel, Dave, Fuzzy, Mappy Flappy, Scabies Murphy,
Doctor Octo-Dread, and most of all,
the very merry Mary Rose*

Once in a while you get shown the light
in the strangest of places
if you look at it right.

—Jerry Garcia & Robert Hunter

These poems were sold
On Shakedown Street
One for five
Or three for ten

—Hustling Words

Brother can you spare a crime?
My 1969
VW marshmallow
Broke down
Outside of Hard Knoxville
And I got nowhere to go
Except for inside out

—Looking to Score

Remember all them kids who died
Doing what they love

—Freebird

Skyler added a hundred thousand miles per year
To his rainbow tie-dyed school bus
Chasing after the electric hive-soul of his tribe

He knew the USA's highways
As if he paved them all himself
With liquid sunshine

Miracles happened to him every day
And he expected them to continue

—Proud to be a High School Dropout

He traded church
For concerts

Concerts got him higher
Closer to the light

Band and fans all melting together
He would lose himself
In the hive vibe

—The Sonic Rapture

"Pshhhhhhhhh!"
The siren sings to us

"Ice-cold balloons! Get your ice-cold balloons!"

We free our wallets
Hoping to fill our bottomless souls
With echoing laughter

The streets are painted pointillistic
With flaccid discarded balloons

—Kaleidoscopic Wasteland

They ate some mushrooms

And smoked a fatty

In the parking lot

Before they went inside the show

To smoke another fatty

And eat more mushrooms

—Ready for Takeoff

Her name wasn't really Crystal Haze
His name wasn't really Shaman Shawn

Wake & Bake was their daily mantra
They began their mornings with sativa
They ended their nights with indica

They had drugs and music in common
That was enough for them

They didn't need anything else to talk about

—*Plastic Day-Glo Peace Signs*

She gave him a rose
He got her drunk
She gave him another rose
He got her high
She gave him a third rose
He asked for a loan
She gave him her fourth rose
He got her hooked
On thorns
Stealing the fifth rose
For someone else
And never looked back

It's okay
She told herself
There were still seven lucky roses left
In her bouquet
And when those were gone
She could always gather
What others had lost
Or steal someone else's

—Dead Roses

It was like time-travelling

Back to the days of cavemen

Dozens of wooly neo-Neanderthals

Gathered in a circle

In the parking lot

Banging on drums

Howling

To keep the deadly future at bay

Inside the drum circle

Bodies writhed and capered

Some possessed by spirits of asphalt

Others flaunting their bare joy

Making even the angels blush

—Tuning in the Ancients

The typical stench of the city
Was temporarily overpowered
By herbaceous sage and musky patchouli
Cheap strawberry incense mingling
With hundred-dollar clouds
Of marijuana smoke
And the honest sweat of deadheads
At the end of a long tour

—Magic in the Air

Jungle, forest, desert, beach—
Nature is the profoundest place
For an acid test

That being said
If you're at a crowded concert
And you want to fly cosmically high
Here's some advice:

Don't

But if you must
Only score from friends you trust

Drop the liquid lightning
Chew the bittersweet flesh of the gods
Lick the paper's secret wisdom
Half an hour before the show

Have a preorbital adventure
Finding your seats
Or better seats if any are available
Smoke 'em if you got 'em
Wait for things to get weird

And if the rollercoaster dragon takes you
To the edge of the abyss…

Don't fight it
Don't resist
It's only the drug
It's only you

Follow it through

To be reborn
Your ego must first die

Avoid looking at yourself in mirrors
Avoid thinking about yourself
Avoid yourself in general
You'll only get in your own way

Remember to breathe

"Be here now," preaches Ram Dass

"You can be anyone this time around," preaches Timothy Leary

"Life flows on within you and without you," preaches the Beatles

"You reached for the secret too soon," preaches Pink Floyd

"If you get confused, listen to the music play," preaches the Grateful Dead

"Everything's right so just hold tight," preaches Phish

Surrender to the flow
Let the music be your guide
Not the musicians

Let the fractal waves wash over you
And deliver you where they may

You'll soon enter
The warm molasses intrauterine phase
Of the trip
Freed from your former world's anxieties
Death-defying
And born anew

—Brainwashing 101

Faces warp
Bizarre and scary
When the lights come on
After the show
Faces painted with happy, vacuous expressions
None of us look real
As if we're all just
Trying our best
To pretend we're human

Outside the arena
Grizzled burnouts abound everywhere
My curious third eye wanders
Bad trip husks of hunters too old
To chase their dreams over the Bifrost
Stuck in a permanent flashback

—*Show's Over, Folks*

Bodhisattva Jerry Garcia died of a heart attack
August 9, 1995
An overweight heroin addict with diabetes
Wasn't the wisest bet for immortality
Regardless of how many worshipers
Wished otherwise
Caravan culture hit the brakes
There was a ten thousand car pileup on the rainbow road
That day
Kaleidoscopic pools of blood spilt everywhere
And the vinyl groove faded to a digitized memory

—Tripping Over Rainbows

The Family believed Jerry Garcia
Was an incarnation of the Hindu god Vishnu
They refused to look directly at him
Inside the concerts
They spun for hours in trancelike prayer
Behind the stage
Dozens of red-eyed roses garbed in psychedelic petals
Twirling 'round and 'round
In a Wonderland flower garden

Big Crawdaddy bobbed his head and swayed his arms
And sometimes did the pogo
But he never danced
His rhythmic movements were more spastic
Than graceful
He tried mimicking the spinners once—
Everything became a passing blur
The furious whirling filtered out the world
Only letting the music seep through
He surrendered to the flow
But the flow quickly overtook him
Making him dizzy

Unbalancing him

He stumbled and tripped mid a cluster of the cultists

Causing a domino effect of spinners stepping on toes

And bumping into wooks

Bouncing off each other like whirligigs

Or dreidels

In a mosh pit

—The Church of Unlimited Devotion

Hustling to scalp his extra ticket for twice its worth
And here comes Smiley Kylie
Waving her finger in the wintry gray sky
Hoping for a miracle

She looked so sweet
And he felt so high
How could he resist?

A kiss on the cheek
As payment in fool
And off she twirled
To find her makeshift family
Inside the concert

—Hypnotized by Tie-Dyed Butterflies

All the hairy monsters
Who earned their living by selling daydreams
On Shakedown Street
Were his loyal friends
Though nobody knew his real name
Mister Pink belonged to a guild of outlaw chemists
Called *The Alternative*

The fish were hungry
And Mister Pink had the bait they craved
Rocketship to godhead
Shortcut to Nirvana
Also called lysergic acid diethylamide
A lifetime of meditation on the mountaintop
Could not yield the transformative experience
Of a 200 microgram dose of LSD

Mister Pink believed everyone on the planet
Should take LSD at least once
Just to experience firsthand the illusory nature
Of their world

Less than ten seconds to make the nervous exchange
A hundred perforated hits of pure freedom
And off dashed Mister Pink
With his wild plan to overthrow the government
One dose at a time

—Chemical Rebellion

Brother Josiah
Was a gluten-intolerant vegan
Who refused to eat anything
That had been cooked or frozen
Or genetically modified
Or artificially colored
Or artificially flavored
Or processed in any manner whatsoever

Most of his life
Revolved around
Planning meals
And scoring heroin

—Greasy Grilled Cheese Sandwiches!

1½ cups of canna-butter
3 cups of oats
¼ cup of peanut butter
3 tablespoons of honey
2 teaspoons of cinnamon
2 tablespoons of cocoa powder
A pinch of freedom
A dash of rebellion

Melt the canna-butter in a microwave. Take a bong hit. In a large bowl, combine the oats, peanut butter, honey, cinnamon, and cocoa. Take a bong hit. Then think about the first time you got high. Who were you with, and why? Pour the canna-butter into the mixture and stir until you find peace with the decisions you've made in life, or the mixture becomes uniform, whichever occurs first. Take a bong hit. Cool the mixture in a freezer for 10-20 minutes, using a 15-minute performance of "Dark Star" from Winterland '74 as your timer. Take a bong hit. Form the mixture into individuals balls. The balls should resemble your state of mind. Take a bong hit.

—Ganja Goo Balls

Got a bad case of the post-show munchies?
How about some spaghetti
Or lasagna
Made on the spot
In the parking lot?
We have it right here
Amid ice chests with signs
Calling out "buck-a-beer!"

We have the *Veggie Burrito Boyz*
Working alongside the *Killa Grilla Cheez Ladeez*

We have "da bomb" blitzkrieg crepes
And dreamy creamy wiffle waffles
We even have tabouli and falafels

And if you're really high
Slice the flying eyeball pie
Cut your teeth on a white-knuckle sandwich
Stuff yourself with candied dandies
And butterscotch flimflams
Until you vomit rainbow sprinkles

And if your throat goes dry
Simply look up to the sky
And stick out your tongue
The blue marshmallow clouds
Are raining electric Kool-Aid

Yep, we have it all here
From vegan snark steaks to snozzberry beer
Or perhaps you'd prefer
My fresh hairy berries, 100% organic

—*Pleasure Island Principle*

The Wharf Rats are heads who

Do not drink

Do not smoke

Do not trip

And bathe regularly

On Mars

Humans are the aliens

—Same Tribe, Different Vibe

Some deadheads took their brand of nonsense seriously
Others found it hard to take anything seriously at all
Mostly it depended on what drugs they were into

—Prankster for Life

By the time you went to three hundred Dead shows

You knew the names of everyone else

Who had gone to three hundred Dead shows

Or more—

The tribal elders and rainbow warriors

The tie-dyers and glassblowers

The Family

The Wrecking Crew

Even the Nitrous Mafia

And you probably shared a spliff

Or banged a conga

With most of the greenhorns

(Anyone who had been to less concerts than you)

—Urban Nomads

After a hundred sonic pilgrimages
Any enterprising soul could spot a custie*
From a parking lot away
They were easy to distinguish—
Frat boys looking to score a bag of killer weed
Wannabe hippy throwbacks from the sixties
Wearing glow-in-the-dark peace signs
Hoping to make up for that chance
They missed out on in college
Because they were too uptight to inhale
Punk rockers, hip-hoppers, teenyboppers
Blonde salon dreadlocks
Hell's Angels angling to capitalize
On your moment of weakness
Underground businessmen worried about
Getting ripped off
For a bunk sheet of acid

—Buyer Beware!

---

*Custie: Pejorative slang for *customer*, especially one who can be charged significantly more than the going price. If you needed to read this definition in order to understand the word *custie*, you are most likely a custie.

We call them trustafarians

We call them wooks

We call them wingnuts & kooks

We call them custies

We call them crusties

We call them drainbows & musty old fusties

Believing we're more openminded

Than our parents

—Mind Your Own Party

Erica's hundredth show was only fifty-three miles away
A very momentous occasion
The worn-out soles of her Birkenstock sandals
Reminded her
Of a thousand adventures she could hardly believe
And some she could barely remember

Everyone who joined the traveling circus
Had a headful of unbelievable tales
That were true
Well, mostly true

—Fractal Highways

All they ever listened to were live recordings
Of Grateful Dead concerts
They had hundreds of bootleg tapes
Rare acquisitions like the Muir Beach acid test
And the Egypt concerts of '78
Some of their tapes only played the same song
Over and over
But from different shows

The Grateful Dead performed 2,314 "official" concerts
Between 1965 and 1995*

A forty-six minute version of "Playing in the Band"
Is the longest continuous song the Dead ever played

"Playing in the Band" also happens to be
The Dead's most played (played-out?) song
Making 678 live appearances

—Most Deadheads are Amateur Historians

---

*Rebranding as Dead & Company after the death of Jerry Garcia.

Some lyrics don't mean what you think
Even the ones that do, don't
Careful what you invest
Reality in, because
Entertainment machines care more for your money
Than your health, and
Some lyrics don't mean what they say

Absolute truth cannot
Be bought
Or sold into copyrighted slavery
United we stand
Never mind the fine print
Divided we fall

—*Sometimes the Set List Hides Secret Messages*

Slick Johnson sold tiny paper tabs of LSD
To custies
Crouching down between parked cars
In the concert venue parking lots
Wherever Shakedown Street manifested

There are a hundred tabs in a sheet of acid
Mister Pink charged Slick fifty dollars per sheet
And Slick retailed each individual tab
For five dollars

This is how Slick earned enough money
To tour around the country
Without having a real job

—Whoring the Divinity

His cardboard sign pleads
Spread some cheddar on this broke cracker

We didn't sign the contract of civilization
To keep living paw-to-maw like brute animals
We signed up to prosper

So where's the prosperity?

—The King of All Cons

Dogs roam the parking lot
With contact highs
Scrounging for whatever's left

"Get that mutt off my purebred!"

Prowling and growling and barking and
Biting and fighting and fucking shamelessly
Begging for scraps at the food stalls

"Go away! Shoo! Ain't nothing here for you!"

Some are strays
Others simply unattended
Faithful hounds to faithless masters

—Lot Dogs

An ambulance drove onto the scene
A blaring intruder from the foreign world
Of mortgages and five o' clock deadlines
Outside the traveling bubble of dreamland

Paramedics were here
To calm down some wigged-out tripper
A girl screaming about how she was unable to breathe
Though her bellowing proved contrary

Then the cops pulled up
The girl was hauled away in handcuffs
She was probably just having a bad trip
Now it was about to get a lot worse

Slick Johnson hoped she didn't purchase
Her nightmare from him
He had dealt to so many strangers throughout the day
Nobody could remember all their faces

—Casualties of Peace

Spring tour, summer tour, fall tour, winter tour, repeat
The Dead never stop playing
So the diehards never stop touring
East Coast concerts at the Knickerbocker Arena
In New York
Midwest concerts at the Deer Creek Music Center
In Indiana
West Coast concerts at the Oakland Coliseum
In California
And the road
Always focusing on the road ahead
All roads lead to Shakedown Street
The eighth wonder of the uncivilized world:
33% black market
33% electrified mysticism
33% Martian
And 1% indescribable chaos
Anything can be bought or bartered
Magic beans and elven rings
Flying carpets chartered
Complete with *Psilocybe* sherpas
On Shakedown Street

An interdimensional fun zone

Populated with time-traveling prophets

Dreadlocked ascetics

Doomsday fortunetellers

Guitar-strumming gurus

Crystal-hawking stargazers

And sometimes

Late at night

When everyone is really fucked up

Bacchus or Pan might even make an appearance

With a frolicking retinue of centaurs and satyrs

—Shakedown Street

& panhandling pirates & psychedelic clowns & glittery faerie folk & white witches & rainbow wizards & Big Lebowskis & Buddha-esque Bukowskis & "Jah Rastafari!" appropriators & wrinkly nudist sunbathers & poorly disguised lizard men & sasquatches with bright ribbons in their hair & angels with broken wings & red-eyed lop-eared rabbits smoking blunts & Slick Johnson selling blotter to the Devil himself &

—On Safari

I was trying to sneak my glass pipe into the show
When it fell on the pavement and broke
That'll be the third pipe this tour

Our most prized Pyrex paraphernalia
Are blown by Bob Snodgrass the Third
A master craftsman from Eugene, Oregon
His father, Bob Snodgrass the Second
Was an expert glassblower
As was his father's father, Bob Snodgrass prime
Bob's been apprenticing his son lately
Bob Snodgrass the Fourth*

Deadheads consider Snodgrass pipes and bongs
Priceless objets d'art
Galaxies fumed in gold and silver
Swirling 'round their heady nugs

***—I Paid $850 for My Bubbler
and It Broke Two Weeks Later***

---

*Bob Snodgrass the Fourth grew up and had a son of his own,
Bob Snodgrass the Fifth, who is carrying on the family
tradition of glassblowing.

Smuggling the hopeful spirit of the sixties
Into the cynical decade of the nineties
The Grateful Dead didn't just have fans
They had lifelong worshippers

After Jerry Garcia reawakened
From a diabetic coma in 1986
Rumors spread of his resurrection

—Following in the Footsteps

Gideon thought the Dead rocked
Sometimes
But this was not why he followed them
From state to state
Across the country

He followed the Band of the Dead
To escape his hometown of Nowhereville, Illinois
Touring with the Dead was sort of like running away
And joining a circus
Finding a purpose
Being part of a real family

—Phamily Comes in Different Flavors

Experts at tricks of their trade
The Church of Unlimited Devotion (a.k.a. The Family)
Managed to sneak into almost every concert venue
Across America
Using bunk tickets and Jedi mind tricks

If any disciple failed to get in
None of the Family would enter
That particular concert-cum-mothership
They understood the importance of community
As cultists often do

—*The Family Ended in Scandal, As Cults Often Do*

When Timothy Leary preached
Turn on, tune in, drop out
We should have known
He really meant
Turn in, tune out, drop a dime
In the newest collection plate

—No More Gurus

A free ticket is a miracle
And miracles are real

A used ticket
Taped or glued back together
Is a tricket

Two different ticket ends
Taped or glued together
Is a twicket

A fast pass is just a $20 bill
And a friendly wink

Counterfeit isn't what it appears
The ignoblest and most honest of arts

Handing the ticket taker a used stub
Or a grocery store receipt
As you freely pass
Is a Jedi mind trick

Of course you can always try to
Rush the gate

Or beat up a scalper

—Ticketmaster Prices Are for Suckers

There was another type of weirdo
Who frequented Dead shows—
Undercover cops
Networks of them
Always sniffing around
Causing trouble for the lifers
They had extensive dossiers on everyone
Who was anyone in the scene
Including me

Prison sentences for LSD
Are based on the weight of the material
Used to distribute the drug:
Blotting paper, sugar cubes, a pitcher of Kool-Aid
Not the actual weight of the drug itself

—The CIA Says Hello

Slick Johnson had dozens of connections

Way more connections than friends

Oftentimes the roles overlapped

—*Just Say No?*

From one to one hundred shows
It was all about shrooms and LSD

From one hundred to two hundred shows
It was all about coke and molly

From two hundred to three hundred shows
It was all about Special K and chasing the dragon

From three hundred shows onward
It was all about love and light

—Enlightenment or Die

The Pied Pipers of Haight-Ashbury
Are coming to your town
Gonna show all the bad kids
Just what's going down

Them kids, they come a running
To jump on board the bus
Anxious to leave the webs small towns weave
Before their mettle goes to rust

Slip loose
Break free
However the hell you can
Get your ass down to Candyland

—Take the Tie-Dyed Pill

They overtook the city
Claiming squatter's rights
They bathed in the public fountains
Filling the parks with teepees and yurts

They took the doors off all the houses
And used them to build new houses

Some of them set up camp in supermarkets
Others laid their sleeping bags down
In liquor stores
And libraries

They seeded the asphalt
Turning the streets into victory gardens

They crocheted rainbow-colored sweaters
For the trees
And painted brightly-colored murals
On the barren walls

They freed the prisoners
And locked up the politicians

They looted the banks
And burned all the money
Trading cannabis for craftmanship
Bartering time, muscle, and know-how

But their main currency was gossip
And they were rich in it

—Deadland

The usual cast of Learys & Owsleys were
Playing their games and plying their trades
On the lot

Hey now, there's Wavy Gravy the tie-dyed clown
And his Hog Farm crew
And over there's Kesey and his famous Further bus
A revolution on wheels
And there's Fast Eddie making a quick buck
And there's Harry Perry, turban and everything
Roller-skating up and down the aisles
Jamming on his electric guitar
And Blueblood Benson giving newbies the eye
    Pegleg Dan bumming a smoke on the fly
    Bearded Betty peddling organic apple pie
(She used to be a fashion model
Before joining the psychedelic circus and
Swearing off razors)
And Stagger Lee staggering
    Cosmic Charlie swaggering
    Tennessee Jed wishing he were dead
    Loose Lucy acting all goosey

And Dorothy & Alice
  Mad Hatter & March Hare
    Cheshire Cat & Cat in the Hat
      The Egg Man & the Walrus
        And the court jester
          And the village idiot
            And the tarot card fool
          And the falafel guy
          And the *Killa Grilla Cheez Ladeez*
        And the ganja goo balls
      And the nitrous tanks
    And the promise of *The Sonic Rapture*
  And all the kids looking for one last adventure
Before the end of the world

—*Portrait of a Dead Scene, 1989*

J. Martin Strangeweather is a veteran of the psychedelic circus road. An expert tightrope walker and mental contortionist, his clown-sage teardrops have lately all been turning to fool's gold. He currently has two other collections of poems available: *Poems from the Polka-Dot Apocalypse* (Four Feathers Press), and *Poems from the Dayglow Slaughterhouse* (Weird Roach Productions).

www.ingramcontent.com/pod-product-compliance
Lightning Source LLC
Chambersburg PA
CBHW032017290426
44109CB00013B/689